Audition Songs for Female Singers 2

I Will Always Love You...

plus ten more essential audition standards

This book © Copyright 2004 by Amsco Publications,
A Division of Music Sales Corporation, New York
All Rights Reserved.

Order No. AM 981167
ISBN 0.8256.3331.1

Exclusive Distributors:
Music Sales Corporation
257 Park Avenue South
New York, NY 10010 USA.

Music Sales Limited
8/9 Frith Street,
London W1D 3JB, England.

Music Sales Pty Limited
120 Rothschild Avenue,
Rosebery, NSW 2018, Australia.

www.musicsales.com

Printed in United States of America by
Vicks Lithograph and Printing Corporation

Amsco Publications
A Part of The Music Sales Group
London/New York/Paris/Sydney/Copenhagen/Berlin/Tokyo/Madrid

...Baby One More Time

Words and Music by Max Martin

Verse 2:
Oh baby, baby
The reason I breathe is you.
Boy, you got me blinded.
Oh pretty baby
There's nothing that I wouldn't do.
It's not the way I planned it.

Show me how you want it to be   *etc.*

Big Spender

Music by Cy Coleman. Lyric by Dorothy Fields.

wouldn't you like to know what's go - ing on in my mind? So let me get

right to the point, I don't pop my cork for ev - 'ry man I see.___

___ Hey big spen - der,

spend_____ a lit - tle time___ with me.

9

Black Velvet

Words and Music by Christopher Ward and David Tyson

1. Mis - sis - sip - pi in the mid - dle of a dry___ spell,___
(Verse 2 see block lyric)

Jim - my Rog - ers___ on the Vic - tro - la up high,___

Ma - ma's danc - ing___ with a ba - by___ on her shoul - der,___

the sun is set - ting like___ mo - las - ses___ in the sky.___

The boy could sing,__ knew__ how to move ev - 'ry - thing.____

Al - ways want - ing more,__ he'd leave you long - ing for

Black Vel - vet and that lit - tle boy's__ smile,___

Black Vel - vet with that slow south - ern style, a new re - li - gion__ that - 'll

ooh, hoo._____ In a flash__ he was gone,__

It hap - pened_so__ soon._____ What could you do?____

(Guitar solo)

18

Verse 2:
Up in Memphis, the music's like a heatwave
White lightning, bound to drive you wild.
Mama's baby is in the heart of every schoolgirl
"Love Me Tender" leaves 'em crying in the aisle.
The way he moved, it was a sin, so sweet and true.
Always wanting more, he'd leave you longing for...

Black Velvet *etc.*

I'm Not A Girl, Not Yet A Woman

Words and Music by Dido Armstrong, Max Martin, and Rami Jacoub

Verse 2:
I'm not a girl
There is no need to protect me
It's time that I, learn to face up to this
On my own
I've seen so much more than you know now
So don't tell me to shut my eyes.

I'm not a girl *etc.*

Hopelessly Devoted To You

Words and Music by John Farrar

eyes are not the first to_____ cry._____ I'm

not the first to know there's just no get-ting ov — — er

you._____ 2. I

know I'm just a fool who's_____ will - ing_____ to

head is say - ing "Fool, for - get him."_____ My

I Will Always Love You

Words and Music by Dolly Parton

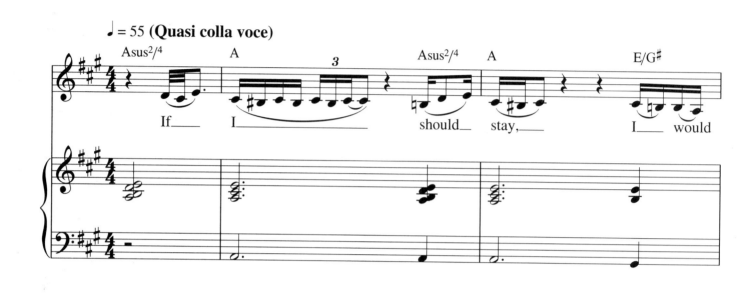

think of you___ ev-'ry step_ of the way.___

a tempo (♩ = 60)

And I_____ will al - ways

love you,_____ I____ will al - ways

poco accel.

love you,_____ you,_____ my

If My Friends Could See Me Now

Music by Cy Coleman. Lyric by Dorothy Fields.

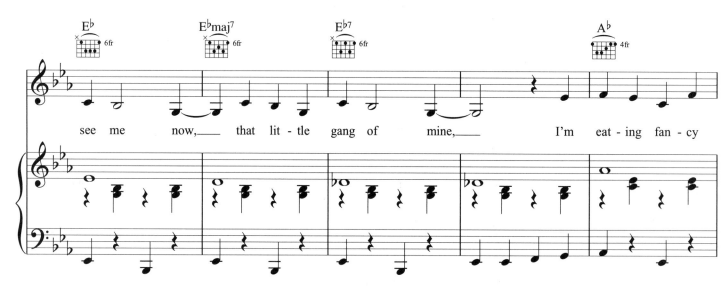

Let's Play A Love Scene

Music by Steve Margoshes. Lyrics by Jacques Levy.

Miss Byrd

Music by David Shire. Lyrics by Richard Maltby, Jr.

But I know some-thing that peo - ple don't know.

Ev - 'ry - one who sees___ me thinks___ That I'm that dull Miss Byrd.

(Verse 3 see block lyric)

___ I could blow that myth___ a - part,___ But

47

49

51

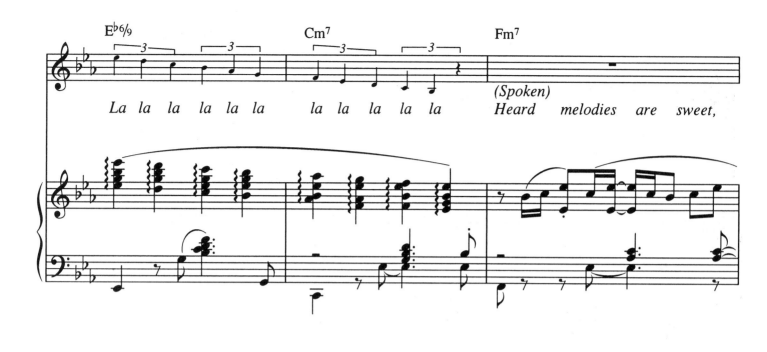

La la la la la la   la la la la la   *(Spoken)*
Heard melodies are sweet,

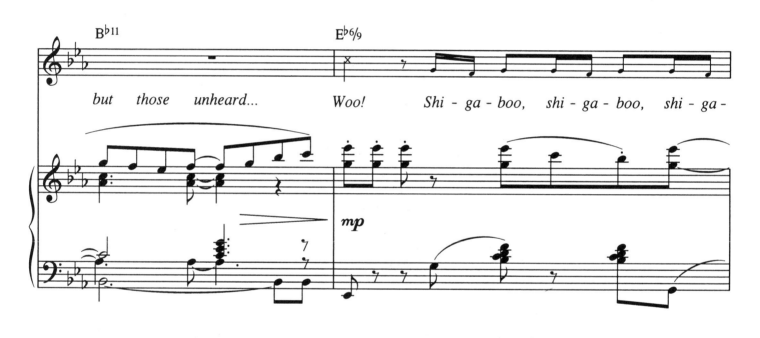

but those unheard... Woo! Shi - ga - boo, shi - ga - boo, shi - ga -

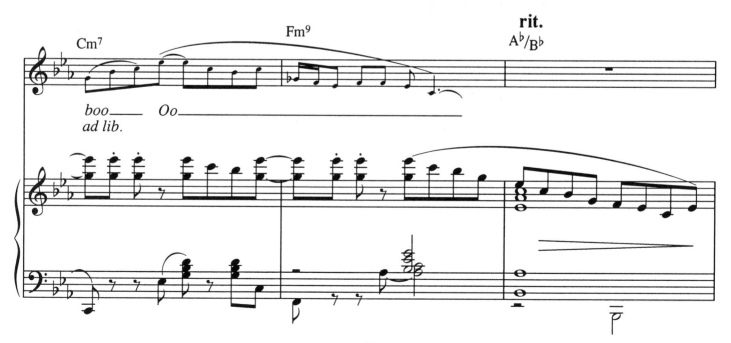

boo___ Oo_____
ad lib.

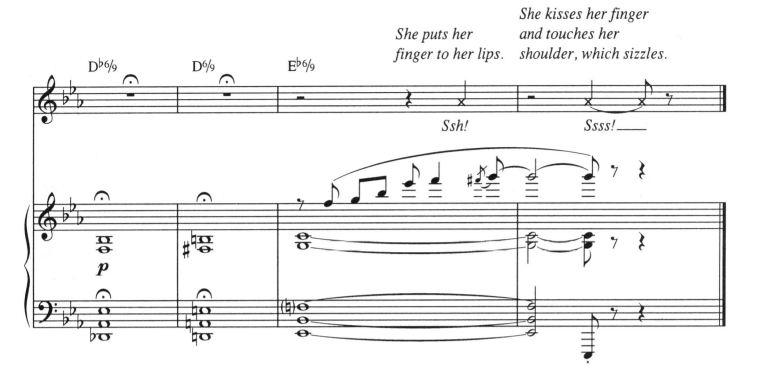

Verse 2

Down in Apartment 'A', the Super's aptly named.
Last week I went to the basement more hours than I claimed.
He says I'm super, too; he calls me hot.
I show those basement apartments a lot!
Back at work I'm crisp and fresh, reliable Miss Byrd.
Seals are dancing in my flesh, but I don't say a word.
I'm showing Penthouse 'C'; as I begin,
I still feel his hands sliding over my skin.
My nipples start to throb inside my bra;
That's when I start to go "Lah dah di dah".
If you've never felt the lift a little lunch can bring,
This bird is singing; Miss Byrd is singing.
I'm singing "I'm on fire!", but I'm not saying a thing.

Verse 3

Lots of girls who first seem shy have secrets, I have found.
If you think I'm special, I suggest you look around.
That little office temp who seems so dumb,
How come a trip to MacDonald's is making her hum?
And Mrs Smith in Sales, who's turning grey,
Why is she smiling that curious way?
If it's true the drabbest song-birds come alive in Spring,
The birds are singing; Miss Byrd is singing.
I'm singing "I'm in love!", but I'm not saying a thing.

You Can Always Count On Me

Music by Cy Coleman. Lyrics by David Zippel.

right,   but what good does it do me a-lone on a Sat-ur-day   night?

Easy swing (♩ = 96)

I   don't need   a   map,   I nat - 'ral - ly head for the
mat - ter   of fact,   if   you want an ill - fat - ed
my   kind   of dame no doubt will die out like the

dead end   street.__   You can al - ways count on   me.__   I'm
love af - fair,__   you can al - ways count on   me.__   Though
di - no - saurs,__   you can al - ways count on   me.__   I'm

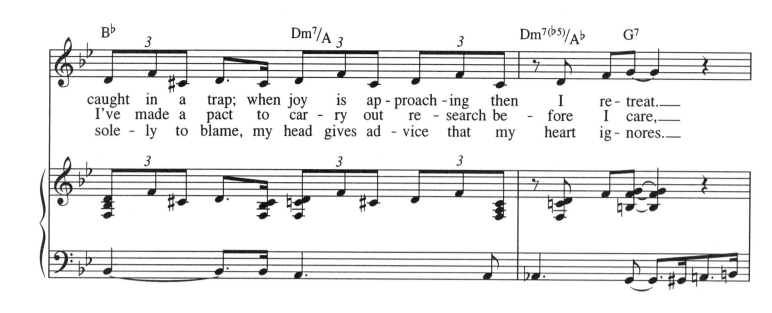

caught in a trap; when joy is ap - proach - ing then I re - treat.___
I've made a pact to car - ry out re - search be - fore I care,___
sole - ly to blame, my head gives ad - vice that my heart ig - nores.___

I'm at home with mis - er - y.___ I've
men don't give a war - ran - ty.___ One
I'm my on - ly en - e - my.___ I

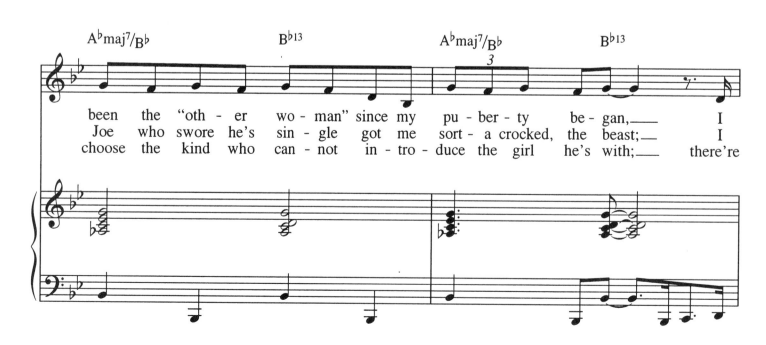

been the "oth - er wo - man" since my pu - ber - ty be - gan,___ I
Joe who swore he's sin - gle got me sort - a crocked, the beast;___ I
choose the kind who can - not in - tro - duce the girl he's with;___ there're

crashed the jun - ior prom and met the on - ly____ mar - ried man.____ I'm
woke up on - ly slight - ly shocked that I'd de - frocked a priest.____ Or
lots of smirk - ing mo - tel clerks who call me____ Miss - us Smith,____ but

al - ways on top for ro - mance or choc -'late that's bit - ter - sweet.____
else I at - tract the guys who are long - ing to do my hair.____
I've made a name with ho - tel de - tect - ives who break down doors.____

To Coda

You can al - ways count on me.____ A ____
You can al - ways count on me.____

I

go for the riff - raff who's treat - ing me so— so; when I can play the se - cond fid - dle

I'm a vir - tu - o - so. I should be play - ing for a wed - ding band, but

there're no wed - ding rings at - tached,— though

you can bet there're strings at - tached.——— Though

CODA

Guess who they ex - pect to see?__ You can al - ways count on,

bet a large a - mount on, you can al - ways count on me!__

cresc. to end

f

59

Take Me To Your Heart (La Vie En Rose)

Original French Lyrics by Edith Piaf. English Translation by Frank Eyton. Music by Louiguy.

Il me l'a dit me l'a ju - ré_____ pour la vi - e. Et dès que je a-per-
ev - 'ry day words seem to turn_____ in - to love songs. Give your heart and soul to

-çois, a - lors je sens en moi, mon coeur qui bat.
me and life will al - ways be la vie en rose.

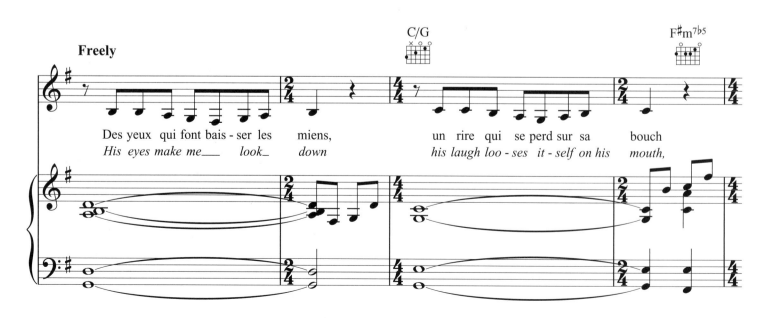

Des yeux qui font bais - ser les miens, un rire qui se perd sur sa bouch
His eyes make me___ look_ down his laugh loo - ses it - self on his mouth,